Hurricanes

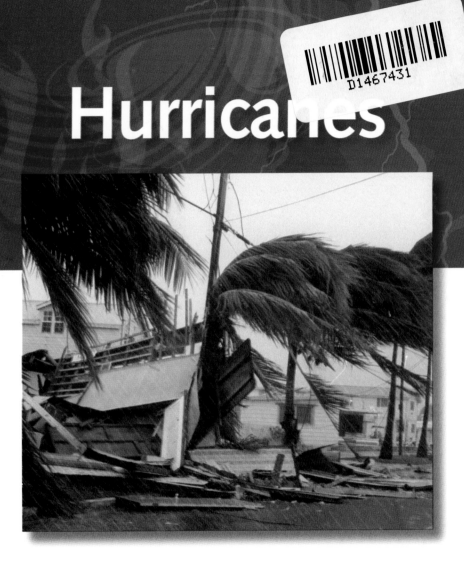

William B. Rice

Hurricanes

Publishing Credits

Associate Editors
James Anderson
Torrey Maloof

Editorial Director
Dona Herweck Rice

Editor-in-Chief
Sharon Coan, M.S.Ed.

Creative Director
Lee Aucoin

Illustration Manager
Timothy J. Bradley

Publisher
Rachelle Cracchiolo, M.S.Ed.

Science Consultant
Scot Oschman, Ph.D.

Teacher Created Materials

5301 Oceanus Drive
Huntington Beach, CA 92649-1030
http://www.tcmpub.com
ISBN 978-1-4333-0312-8
© 2010 Teacher Created Materials, Inc.

Table of Contents

The First Hurricane

Mayan legend from long ago tells of a powerful **weather** god. He ruled the winds and storms. To create the Earth, he endlessly chanted, "Earth, Earth, Earth!" At last, the world rose up from the sea.

The story goes on. The people of Earth did not do what all the gods said to do. The gods became angry. The powerful storm god let loose winds and rain unlike any that had been seen before. The terrible storm killed all the people.

Today, we name storms such as these after the fierce storm god. He was called Huracan. The storm is called a hurricane.

This is an image of the god Huracan, from an ancient Mayan vase

Hurricane Iris smashes into Belize in 2002.

What Is Weather?

Weather is made of these four elements:

wind: moving air

visibility: how much and how far can be seen through the air with the eye

precipitation: water from the air in the form of rain, snow, or hail

temperature: how hot or how cold the air is

What Is a Hurricane?

A hurricane is a huge storm. It is made of fierce winds that start over the ocean. A hurricane is violent. It can do great damage over a large area.

To know what makes a hurricane, you must first know about wind. Wind is made by the power of the sun. The sun heats the Earth. But the sun does not heat all parts of the Earth the same. Some parts are heated more. The warmest parts of Earth's surface heat the air above them the most. As warm air rises, cooler air rushes in below it. This quick-moving air is the wind.

As air rises, it cools. As it cools, it falls. The cycle of air movement keeps going as warm air rises and cool air rushes in beneath it. The faster this happens, the bigger the wind.

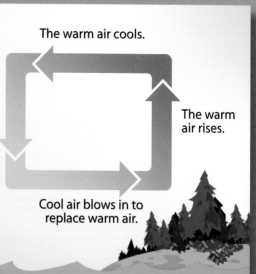

Warm air rises, pulling in cooler air to take its place. The rising air cools and falls back towards Earth's surface.

The warm air cools.

The cool air sinks.

The warm air rises.

Cool air blows in to replace warm air.

This diagram shows the wind cycle.

Wind can be gentle like this breeze that moves prayer flags in Nepal. But at its most powerful, it forms a hurricane.

4 Winds flow outward above the storm. Warm, moist air rises up.

1 A tropical storm comes in.

3 Winds from different directions come together.

Recipe for a Hurricane

What does it take for a hurricane to form? The basic ingredients are warm water, moist air, and strong winds that come together from different directions.

2 Warm ocean water evaporates and creates moist, warm air.

Hurricanes form in ocean **tropics**. These are the warm areas close to Earth's **equator**. Hurricanes begin as tropical waves. These can grow to become tropical depressions, then tropical storms, and finally hurricanes. They start in areas where the ocean water is at least 27°C (80°F). This is where they get their heat and energy.

The tropical storm moves over an area of warm and moist rising air. The warm ocean water **evaporates**. It rises and expands. Cool air rushes in below it. This makes strong winds. The **rotation** of the Earth causes the winds to spin. This is the start of the hurricane.

5

Winds outside the storm push against it. They move the storm and help it grow.

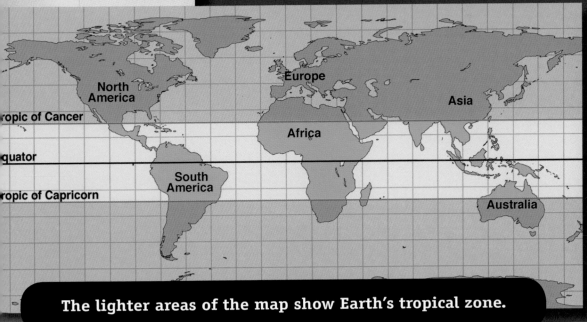

North America

Europe

Asia

Tropic of Cancer

Africa

Equator

South America

Tropic of Capricorn

Australia

The lighter areas of the map show Earth's tropical zone.

In a hurricane, the winds spin around a center called the **eye**. The eye is calm. The air there is clear and the wind is gentle. That is because the spinning motion keeps the rushing winds from coming into the eye. Think of a carnival ride where you stand against the wall of a large, wide tube. The ride spins faster and faster. You are pushed against the wall so hard that you can barely lift your arm or move your head. That is what the spinning storm does, too. It pushes the winds out of the center so that they cannot rush into the middle.

When a hurricane passes by, it will suddenly grow gentle. You may think the storm is over. But this is just the eye. The other half of the hurricane is still to come.

eye of a hurricane

rising warm air

How Big, How Fast, and How Long?

In order to become a hurricane, winds must move at least 119 kilometers (74 miles) per hour. A hurricane may last for more than a week, and it may be hundreds of kilometers in size. Most hurricanes are about 500 kilometers (310 miles) wide. They move about 16–32 kilometers (10-20 miles) per hour across the ocean. As they hit land, they begin to lose strength.

The Better to See You With, My Dear!

The eye of a hurricane is huge! It can stretch from 32–64 kilometers (20–40 miles) across.

descending cold air

eye

eye wall

counterclockwise winds

rain bands

storm surge

hurricane rain bands

Next to the eye are the strongest winds of the hurricane. These are called the **eye wall**. The winds of the eye wall spin fiercely. There may be thunderstorms and tornadoes inside the eye wall.

Rain bands move outward from the eye. They are farther away from the eye than the eye wall is. They move in a circle through the storm. They bring rain into the storm in bands of clouds. Thunderstorms and tornadoes may be in the outer rain bands as well.

'Round and 'Round It Goes

In a hurricane, winds spin counterclockwise north of the equator. They spin clockwise south of the equator. This is due to the Coriolis effect. The Coriolis effect is a natural phenomenon that causes air to curve to the right north of the equator and to the left south of the equator. The Coriolis effect becomes weak near the equator. So no hurricanes can form there.

counterclockwise

clockwise

Hurricane Season

Hurricanes happen during the summer and fall of the year. In the Atlantic Ocean, hurricane season is from June 1 to November 30. In the Eastern Pacific Ocean, it lasts from May 15 to November 30. Most hurricanes happen during the fall.

the eye wall of Hurricane Katrina, before it came ashore

the eye of Katrina

Winds and Hurricane Stages

Hurricanes begin as light winds that are so calm that they barely seem there at all. Then, as they gather strength over the warm ocean water, they become fierce and destructive. To understand winds, a scientist made this scale in 1805. It rates wind strength, speed, class, and effects.

strength = 4

strength = 8

Strength	Speed in Knots
0	less than 1
1	1–3
2	4–6
3	7–10
4	11–16
5	17–21
6	22–27
7	28–33
8	34–40
9	41–47
10	48–55
11	56–63
12	64+

Beaufort Wind Scale

Class	Effects on Water	Effects on Land
m	sea surface smooth	smoke rises straight up
ht air	ripples; no foam	smoke drift shows wind direction; still wind vanes
ht breeze	small wavelets	wind felt on face; leaves rustle; vanes begin to move
ntle breeze	large wavelets	leaves and small twigs move; light flags wave
oderate breeze	small waves; many whitecaps	dust, leaves, and paper lifted; small tree branches move
esh breeze	moderate waves; many whitecaps; some spray	small trees begin to sway
rong breeze	larger waves; whitecaps common; more spray	larger tree branches move
ear gale	sea heaps up; waves very large	whole trees sway; resistance felt walking against wind
le	high waves of greater length; foam blown in streaks	twigs torn from trees; cars pushed slightly while in motion
rong gale	high waves; sea rolls; streaks of foam; spray lowers visibility	slight damage to buildings; tiles blow off roofs
orm	very high waves; sea white with foam; heavy rolling; lowered visibility	not common on land; trees broken or uprooted; high damage to buildings
olent storm	very high waves; foam patches cover sea; visibility more reduced	not on land
urricane	air filled with foam; waves taller than buildings; sea white with spray; very low visibility	not on land

If the conditions are right and the wind grows, so does a hurricane. It grows in stages.

A hurricane may start as a tropical wave. The winds are less than 20 **knots**. There is no **closed circulation**. A closed circulation forms when winds blow around a center of low pressure. (Pressure is caused by the weight of the atmosphere.) The tropical wave can grow or die out.

If the wave grows, it becomes a tropical depression. Thunderstorms come together and winds stay under 34 knots. A closed circulation is created at this stage.

A tropical storm forms when a thunderstorm moves over the closed circulation. Winds reach at least 35 knots. Some damage can be caused by this storm. Most of the damage is from heavy rain.

A hurricane forms when the closed circulation becomes an eye. Winds of at least 65 knots rotate around the eye. Damage is done by the wind and rain. The storm can last for two to three weeks!

tropical wave

tropical depression

tropical storm

Other Names for Hurricanes

Hurricanes are called different things depending on where you are. In the Atlantic Ocean, Eastern Pacific Ocean, and Gulf of Mexico, they are hurricanes. In the Western Pacific Ocean, they are called typhoons. In the Indian Ocean and the Bay of Bengal, they are called cyclones. In Australia, they are called cyclones or willy-willies.

hurricane

Not every hurricane is the same. Each one has a different strength. It can gain strength and grow or lose strength and die out. A special scale ranks the strength of a hurricane. It is the Saffir-Simpson Hurricane Scale.

Two scientists made the scale in 1969. They wanted to give people some idea of the power of each hurricane. A category 1 hurricane does the least damage. A category 5 hurricane can destroy wide areas of land and property. It can cause many deaths as well.

Saffir-Simpson Hurricane Scale

Category	Wind Speed	Damage
1	119–153 km/h (74–95 mph)	minimal
2	154–177 km/h (96–110 mph)	moderate
3	178–209 km/h (111–130 mph)	extensive
4	210–250 km/h (131–155 mph)	extreme
5	251 km/h (156 mph) or higher	catastrophic

Hurricanes by Name

Hurricanes in the Atlantic Ocean are given human names. There are six lists of 21 names each. A different list is used each year. Male and female names switch from A to W, skipping Q and U. If all 21 names are used in a year, the Greek alphabet names the rest. If a hurricane does a lot of damage, its name is never used again. Here are the names for 2009: Ana, Bill, Claudette, Danny, Erika, Fred, Grace, Henri, Ida, Joaquin, Kate, Larry, Mindy, Nicholas, Odette, Peter, Rose, Sam, Teresa, Victor, and Wanda.

The remains of Biloxi-Ocean Springs Bridge after Hurricane Katrina

These satellite photos show before-and-after images of a storm surge following Hurricane Ike's landfall in 2008. Vegetation above water is red and vegetation underwater is green.

5+ miles

before

after

storm surge waves

Storm Surge

Big winds are not the only problem in a hurricane. Hurricanes carry huge amounts of water. This water can cause widespread flooding. Flooding can destroy homes and leave countless people homeless.

Hurricanes gather strength from the water. As a hurricane spins, it pulls up the ocean beneath it. This makes a big bulge of water. The bulge is called a **storm surge**. The hurricane can carry this surge toward the land. The surge can be more than 13 meters (43 feet) tall. That is about the height of a four-story building!

As the hurricane nears the coast, the surge raises the sea level. Winds also create giant waves. All this water has nowhere to go but onto the land. It can easily create a terrible flood.

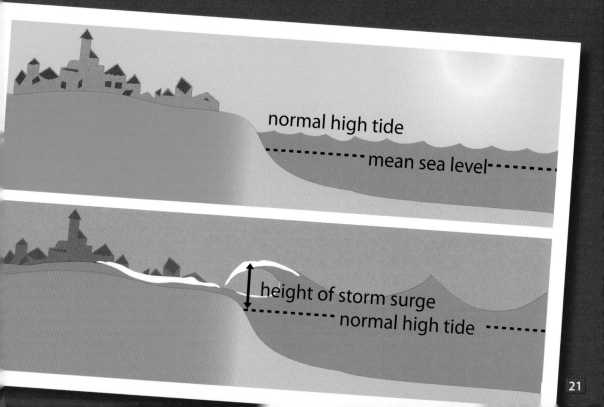

normal high tide

mean sea level

height of storm surge

normal high tide

Small buildings near the shore are covered in water. Boats and other things in the ocean are washed onto the land. Cars and some structures are pulled into the ocean.

The rising water can cause other water bodies to overflow. When this happens, everything nearby becomes flooded. Even after the storm ends, it takes a long time for the water to **recede**. Much damage is left behind. It may take years before things are put right again. Sometimes, they never are.

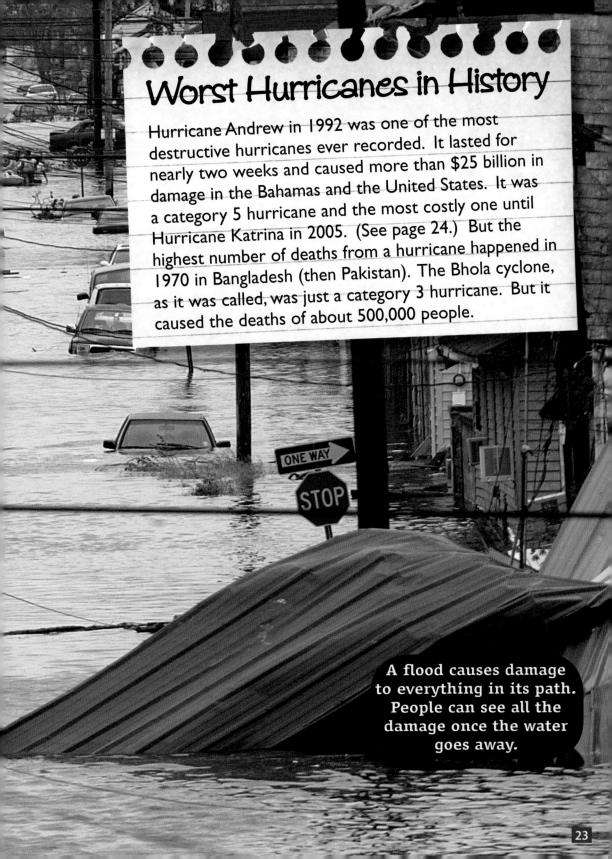

Worst Hurricanes in History

Hurricane Andrew in 1992 was one of the most destructive hurricanes ever recorded. It lasted for nearly two weeks and caused more than $25 billion in damage in the Bahamas and the United States. It was a category 5 hurricane and the most costly one until Hurricane Katrina in 2005. (See page 24.) But the highest number of deaths from a hurricane happened in 1970 in Bangladesh (then Pakistan). The Bhola cyclone, as it was called, was just a category 3 hurricane. But it caused the deaths of about 500,000 people.

A flood causes damage to everything in its path. People can see all the damage once the water goes away.

Hurricane Katrina in 2005 became famous around the world. It began in the Bahamas. Then it crossed to Florida. It began to weaken. But it grew to a category 5 in the Gulf of Mexico. It struck land again along the Gulf Coast. The storm surge it brought caused huge flooding. Even worse, the **levees** around New Orleans failed. More than 80 percent of the city and nearby area were flooded. More than 1,800 people died. At least $81 billion in damage was done.

Scientists had always warned that a levee failure would flood New Orleans. People hoped it would never happen. But it did with Hurricane Katrina.

Hurricane Katrina

Florida

Levee

A levee is a mound of earth or other building material that is built along the banks of a river and is meant to keep high water from flooding onto the land.

dirt levee

This photo shows the Army Corps of Engineers trying to fix a levee break after Katrina.

Technology Today

In the past, the only hurricane warning people had was what they could see themselves. Today, computers and satellites help to predict the effects of a brewing storm and where it may strike. They help us to know how big the storm surge may be. All of this can give people time to prepare and to get out of the way of a hurricane.

Hurricane Hunters

The effects of a hurricane can be terrible. So, people want to know as much about them as they can. In that way, they can be prepared and safe.

Hurricane hunters are scientists. They fly through storms in special planes. They do this to learn about hurricanes. They measure temperature and air pressure. They measure wind speed and direction. The more they know about the hurricane, the more they can tell people.

Hurricanes take a few days to grow. So, people know they are coming. But a hurricane can change direction at any time. You can never be sure which way it will go. It is best to take cover or even leave the area if you think a hurricane is coming your way. Only hurricane hunters should be out in the storm!

Hurricane hunters view the eye wall of Hurricane Katrina from inside the cockpit and outside the plane windows.

Lab: Twister in a Bottl

To see what happens when a funnel is created in a tornado or hurricane, try this experiment. Watch carefully and take some notes about what you see.

Materials
➡ two plastic bottles
➡ duct tape
➡ water

Procedure:

1. Fill one of the bottles about half to three-fourths full with water.

2. Place the open ends of the two bottles together, neck to neck.

3. Securely tape the two necks together by wrapping duct tape around them. Wrap the tape so that it is flat and neat.

4. Turn the bottles over and swirl them so that the water spins through the openings, creating a whirlpool.

5. Watch what happens. What does it tell you about tornadoes and hurricanes?

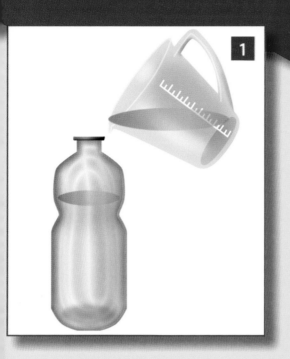

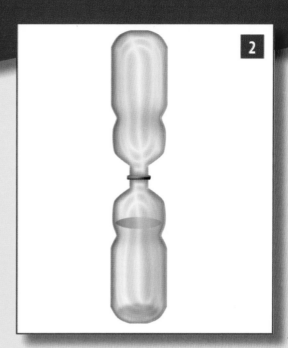

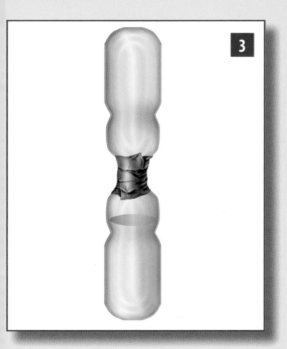

Glossary

closed circulation—an area with winds blowing around a center of low pressure, counterclockwise north of the equator and clockwise south of the equator

equator—an imaginary circle around the Earth that is the same distance from the north and south poles all the way around

evaporates—turns a liquid to a gas or vapor

eye—the calm center of a hurricane

eye wall—the violently windy area in a hurricane that surrounds the eye

knot—one nautical mile per hour on the sea; one knot equals about 1.85 kilometers or 1.15 miles per hour

levee—an embankment built along the edges of a river to keep high water from flooding the land around it

precipitation—water from the air in the form of rain, snow, or hail

recede—to move back, as the tide does

rotation—spinning

storm surge—the swell of water caused by a hurricane that reaches the shore, usually resulting in massive flooding

temperature—how hot or how cold the air is

tropics—the areas of land just above and below the equator

visibility—how much and how far can be seen through the air

weather—the state of the atmosphere

wind—moving air

Index

Scientists Then and Now

John Dalton
(1766–1844)

Jim Cantore
(1964–)

John Dalton is best known for studying atoms. But he also studied weather. He kept a daily journal about the weather patterns in his town from 1787 until 1844! He even used homemade equipment to measure the weather. Many believe it was Dalton's journal that helped bring about the scientific study of weather known today as meteorology.

Jim Cantore is a meteorologist for The Weather Channel. He has been studying the weather since he was a boy. Cantore's classmates used to call him and ask him to predict the weather! Today, he predicts the weather for people all over the world. He helps keep people safe by telling them when and where the next storm will hit.